FOUNTAINS
OF DUBLIN

FOUNTAINS OF DUBLIN

GARY BRANIGAN

The History Press Ireland

Dedicated to my beautiful family

First published 2014

The History Press Ireland
50 City Quay
Dublin 2
Ireland
www.thehistorypress.ie

© Gary Branigan, 2014

British Library Cataloguing in Publication Data.
A catalogue record for this book is available from the British Library.

ISBN 978 1 84588 802 2

Typesetting and origination by The History Press

Contents

Author's Note and Acknowledgements

When many consider cities with a heritage of water features, they will more likely think of locations such as Rome, Paris, or Athens, and rarely, if ever, of Dublin. It may surprise the reader to learn that Dublin possesses hundreds of public fountains and water features, of which approximately eighty are historically and/or artistically important.

The main aim of this book is to celebrate this mostly unknown heritage, provide the necessary information to locate and visit these marvels of sculpture and engineering, and detail the interesting stories behind them.

While this book is not an academic treatise and should not be read as such, an overview of the subject is included in the Introduction, but it is deliberately brief in order to afford more space to the Gazetteer. In visiting these sites the reader will discover that while many are maintained in excellent working order and cleanliness, the majority are unfortunately clearly neglected, in many cases ignored by those charged with their upkeep.

Historians rarely engage in any type of research work without stumbling upon some form of study already undertaken by a predecessor. I would like therefore to express my sincere gratitude to the many people, past and present, for the kind assistance, guidance, and encouragement, received both directly and indirectly, during the compilation of this publication. Research facilities at the National Library of Ireland, Royal Society of Antiquaries of Ireland, and Ordnance Survey Ireland have all been invaluable, and thanks go to the wonderful staff who maintain them. Thanks also to the staff of the Office of Public Works and Dublin City Council, who willingly and generously gave of their time to help whenever they could.

Special mention in particular deserves to go to: Jane Goldberger of the Drinking Fountains Association in the UK; Maximillian Matthews, for research work previously engaged in relation to some of Dublin's monuments; Séighean Ó Draoi, sculptor, for help in assisting in the identification of some of the more obscure materials used in some of the fountains' constructions; David Barrett and John Middleton, for editing and proofreading; Martin Branigan for lending an expert photographic touch from time to time; Ronan Colgan and Beth Amphlett of The History Press Ireland for ongoing assistance during the publication process; Albert Crowley of Fountains and Décor (www.fountains-décor.ie) and Barry Dalby of East West Mapping, who completed the maps for the book, and to whom I owe a significant debt of gratitude.

Thank you to the many others who assisted in various ways in bringing the book to completion.

Finally, words alone cannot express my sincere gratitude and appreciation to Jeannette, Tara, and Aoife, for the love, support, encouragement, and patience they have shown throughout this journey.

Gary Branigan, Dublin, 2014

Introduction

Origins

From the Latin '*Fons*' or '*Fontins*', meaning a source or spring, a fountain is an element of built architecture which pours water into a basin or trough, or alternatively jets it into the air.

Mythological associations and archaeological evidence in various countries have given us a glimpse of the various designs and uses of fountains in history since at least the time of the ancient Greeks.

From the earliest times they have been celebrated as being symbols of life, renewal, wealth, and purity.

Originally, they served a purely functional purpose in providing water for drinking and bathing to the residents of cities, towns, and villages.

A stream of water jetting into the air.

The Supply

Given the brackish and unsuitable nature of Liffey water, much of the original clean water supply to Dublin was provided via a cistern on Thomas Street that was fed by the Poddle and the Dodder rivers. This cistern in turn fed a large marble structure in the region of St Audoen's church known as the City Conduit, St Michael's Pipe, or simply the High Pipe.

The City Conduit divided the main feed into numerous smaller pipes which then supplied water to wealthy homes and institutions, such as Dublin Castle and the various barracks; the width of the pipe being in direct correlation with how much was paid for the supply. The larger the sum paid, the wider the pipe.

This situation did not address the need of the poorer classes, as it benefitted only those of privilege. The supply of drinking water generally available to the poor of Dublin was in those days wholly deficient in both quantity and quality, coming, as it did, primarily from pumps and surface spring wells. The consumption of contaminated water was largely responsible for regular outbreaks of cholera and typhoid among the population of the city. In contrast with the lack of clean drinking water, beer and spirits were in plentiful supply and generally cheap to obtain.

Concern for the health and hygiene of Dublin's citizens led to the creation of the Benevolent Free Fountains Association by Charles Manners, Duke of Rutland, and Sir John Blackquiere. The expansion of the charitable works of the Metropolitan Free Drinking Fountain Association from London to Dublin also occurred at this time.

The aims of the organisations were to provide free water to man and beast and that '… no fountain be erected or promoted by the Association which shall not be so constructed as to ensure by filters, or other suitable means, the perfect purity and coldness of the water'.

The latter association then extended its terms of reference and became the 'Metropolitan Drinking Fountain and Cattle Trough Association' to relieve 'The intense suffering which is experienced by all kinds of animals from thirst in the streets …'. Troughs and dog bowls were added to many drinking fountains.

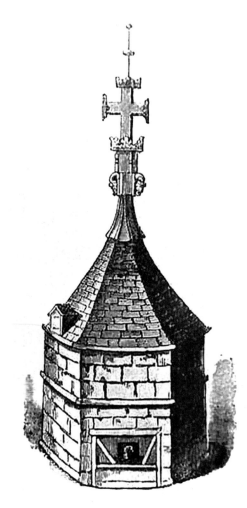

An engraving of the Old City Conduit.

Wealthy benefactors contributed towards the construction of many drinking fountains for the use of both people and animals. They also received huge support from those involved in the temperance movement, concerned as they were with the high levels of alcoholism in the city.

The supply from the City Conduit was extended to the city's fountains.

Logo of the Association.

The Design

Until the late nineteenth century most fountains operated by either of two forces. One needed the structure to be placed over an immediate source of spring water with adequate pressure required to force the water upwards either through the structure into the basin or simply high into the air. Alternatively, a water source was required to be at a sufficient altitude, such as a reservoir or canal, to provide adequate pressure and was carried by way of an aqueduct to make the water flow or jet into the air.

From the mid-twentieth century, as piped water and indoor plumbing were introduced into towns, villages, and cities, fountains become less relevant to everyday life and many became derelict or disappeared, while others became more elaborate and ornamental.

The old trough in Smithfield. The scene of many a horse market.

Dublin County

The remains of a wall-mounted drinking fountain in Fitzwilliam Lane.

Many of the modern fountains were erected to celebrate or commemorate persons or events in history, to decorate public places or grand lawns, or to be focal points in parks and squares.

In more recent times, fountains have become plainer affairs, being simple jets in the centre of stone basins. However, many now have elaborate artwork and/or sculptures erected in association with them.

Visiting fountains has become a favourite pastime for many people across Europe, and specific tours are arranged so people can visit the fountains in various cities and learn of their histories. Dublin is not thought to have anything close to a culture of erecting such monuments, however there are many to see for those who know where to look.

There have been many books written on the topic of fountains and public water features/ mobiles in general and also those which celebrate the monuments that exist in various European cities, but there has been nothing by way of a study on those in any city or town in Ireland.

Unfortunately, the many that exist in Dublin are neglected, vandalised, or simply abandoned. It is hoped that visiting these structures and celebrating our built heritage will encourage the protection of them.

District	Fountain No	Name
North County	1	Stardust Memorial
North County	2	Madonna
North County	3	The Rose Bowl
North County	4	Áras an Uachtaráin
North County	5	St Patrick's College
North County	6	Irish Volunteer
North County	7	Dobby Fin Millen Drill (Nightmare on Duck Street)
North City	8	Battle of the Custom House
North City	9	Children of Lír
North City	10	Gate Theatre
North City	11	Five Lamps
North City	12	Anna Livia
North City	13	Chancery Park
North City	14	Dublin Chamber of Commerce Bicentenary
South City	15	Iveagh Gardens
South City	16	Chariot of Life
South City	17	Crampton Memorial
South City	18	Dáil Éireann
South City	19	Dublin City Rates Office
South City	20	Duke of Rutland Monument
South City	21	Duke of Rutland Memorial
South City	22	' ... for peace comes dropping slow'
South City	23	Edward Stamer O'Grady FRCSI Memorial
South City	24	Fitzwilliam Hall
South City	25	Bord Gáis Energy Theatre
South City	26	South King Street
South City	27	An Garda Síochána Memorial
South City	28	James A. Power Memorial
South City	29	King George II
South City	30	Lady Grattan
South City	31	Leinster Lawn
South City	32	Mansion House
South City	33	Millennium Garden
South City	34	Peace Garden
South City	35	Poddle River
South City	36	Sheahan Memorial
South City	37	Special Olympics

South City	38	Serpent Pool
South City	39	Thomas Davis Memorial
South City	40	The Three Fates
South City	41	Treasury Holdings
South City	42	Veronica Guerin
South City	43	Wilton Plaza
South City	44	Wilton Square
South County	45	Cé a dhéin an domhan? (Who made the world?)
South County	46	Overflow
South County	47	Herbert Park
South County	48	Four Seasons Hotel
South County	49	Rendezvous
South County	50	Bewley's Hotel
South County	51	Ogham Stone
South County	52	Nationwide House
South County	53	Harold's Cross Park
South County	54	St Patrick's Park
South County	55	North South East West
South County	56	Catholic Emancipation Centenary Shrine
South County	57	Farmleigh
South County	58	Islandbridge War Memorial
South County	59	Obelisk
South County	60	People's Garden
South County	61	Oliver Bond
South County	62	Bastard Son of Sisyphus
South County	63	Flock of Mallard Ducks
South County	64	Wave
South County	65	Meeting
South County	66a	Rolling Stones
South County	66b	Homage
South County	67	The Dancing Cranes
South County	68	Dundrum Musical Fountain
South County	69	Marlay House
South County	70	St Enda's Park
South County	71	Usher Memorial
South County	72	Imaginosity
South County	73	Continuum
South County	74	Dún Laoghaire Ferry Terminal

South County	75	People's Park
South County	76	Glencullen
South County	77	Killakee
South County	78	Queen Victoria

Preamble to Gazetteer

The majority of fountains included in this book are located in public or publicly accessible areas. There should not be any difficulty in visiting them during reasonable hours, even for those with mobility issues.

The author has not covered all fountains within the confines of County Dublin, but has instead included all those he deems to be historically relevant and/or artistically important. This extends to fountains with associated artwork.

Flowing water can be a delight to children, but given the very nature of fountains, children should be supervised at all times when playing near them.

Whilst the happy tradition of throwing coins into a fountain is to be expected and celebrated, other additions such as pebbles, washing-up liquid, and litter all damage the internal workings of the structure and are to be avoided.

Many of the fountains in Dublin are in a poor state of repair and the visitor should be prepared to expect some that are highly littered, not functioning, or with stagnant water.

The Gazetteer is divided into five distinct sections. Each section is dedicated to a particular district of County Dublin, and the fountains are listed under each section in alphabetical order by the townland/ward in which they are located. Maps of each district are included for ease of reference.

Ordnance Survey maps or a GPS device can be very beneficial aids in locating these sites, and it would be wise to use these as an accompaniment to this book.

North Dublin County

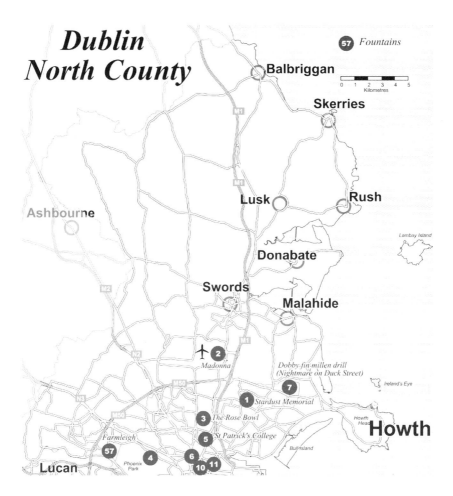

Dublin
North County

57 *Fountains*

Balbriggan

Skerries

0 1 2 3 4 5
Kilometres

Lusk ○   ○ **Rush**

Ashbourne

Lambay Island

Donabate

Swords

Malahide

2
Madonna

Dobby-fin-millen drill
(Nightmare on Duck Street)

Ireland's Eye

7

1 *Stardust Memorial*

3 *The Rose Bowl*

St Patrick's College

5

Howth Head

Howth

Farmleigh

57   **4**

6

10 **11**

Phoenix Park

Bull Island

Lucan

1   Stardust Memorial

Townland/Ward:	Bonnybrook
Latitude, Longitude:	53°23'47.97"N, 6°12'28.85"W
Post Code:	Dublin 5

The Stardust disco in Artane was the scene of a fatal fire which took place in the early hours of St Valentine's Day, 1981. Forty-eight young people died in the fire, with a further 214 being injured. The escape of many was hampered by the failing electrics in the building and the fact that many of the fire exits were obstructed by locks and chains.

The Stardust Memorial, a touching memorial to those young people who lost their lives unnecessarily.

The tragedy devastated the local communities of Artane, Kilmore, and Coolock, and many of the survivors and families have never come to terms with what happened.

A Tribunal of Inquiry held in November of that year concluded that the fire was probably caused by arson. The ruling was firmly disputed by the survivors and was eventually overturned in 2009.

Robin Buick was commissioned by Dublin Corporation in 1993 to create a fitting memorial to the victims of the tragedy, and the Stardust Memorial Park was created. Its central feature is a paved area enclosed by

The unveiling of the monument in 1993. (Image courtesy of Robin Buick)

railings with a moving life-sized bronze sculpture of a boy and girl dancing set into a circular fountain of forty-eight jets spraying, symbolising the number of people who perished that night.

2   Madonna

Townland/Ward: Corballis
Latitude, Longitude: 53°25'43.03"N, 6°14'30.00"W
Post Code: County Dublin

This Madonna fountain was commissioned in 1969 and sculpted by the renowned Imogen Stuart. It is located in the open-air atrium of Our Lady Queen of Heaven church in Dublin Airport.

The Madonna with the modern church spire in the background.

The Madonna fountain situated in the open-air atrium of Our Lady Queen of Heaven church at Dublin Airport.

The Madonna looking up to heaven.

It is comprised of a statue of the Madonna in an alternative form, sculpted in sheet copper. On either side of the square pedestal are small fish spouts from where the water flows.

On the front of the pedestal is the following prayer in block relief:

We fly to thy protection O Holy Mother of God.
Do not scorn our petitions in the hour of need but save us from all perils.
Glorious and Blessed.

3   The Rose Bowl

Townland/Ward: Wad
Latitude, Longitude: 53°23'6.57"N, 6°15'25.58"W
Post Code: Dublin 9

The Rose Bowl was commissioned by the Rose Project for World AIDS Day and unveiled by President Mary McAleese in its original position in St Stephen's Green in 2006.

The fountain, which is also commonly known as the AIDS Memorial Fountain, is dedicated to Rose Atieno, a thirty-two-year-old Kenyan woman who died from the disease in 2003. It also commemorates the many people who have been lost in the AIDS pandemic in Africa.

The Rose Bowl, a unique sculpture to commemorate those who have been taken by the scourge of AIDS in Africa.

The monument was sculpted by Sandra Bell, a self-taught sculptor who uses the lost-wax method for bronze casting and who also incorporates Celtic, Classical, and African influences into her work.

After its pre-agreed term in St Stephen's Green had expired, it was removed and placed into storage until a new home was found was found for it on the Mall in Dublin City University (DCU). It was unveiled in its new location in November 2012 by Kenyan Ambassador, Catherine Muigai Mwangi.

A close-up of the rose.

North Dublin Suburbs

4　Áras an Uachtaráin

Townland/Ward:　　　Castleknock
Latitude, Longitude:　53°21'36.50"N, 6°19'1.42"W
Post Code:　　　　　Dublin 8

This large, formal fountain is located on the lawn in front of the President of Ireland's official residence.

5　St Patrick's College

Townland/Ward:　　　Drishoge
Latitude, Longitude:　53°22'17.67"N, 6°15'18.29"W
Post Code:　　　　　Dublin 9

Dating to the late seventeenth-century, Belvedere House is one of the oldest buildings in Drumcondra and the primary building on the St Patrick's College campus. It was originally built by Sir Robert Booth as a private residence and subsequently purchased by the Vincentian Order in 1883 for conversion into a male-only residential institution for the training of would-be primary school teachers.

The ancient fountain with the former chapel of St Patrick's College in the background.

One of the spouting lion heads.

In the courtyard of the house lies an octagonal tiered limestone fountain with carved lion heads on two levels. Inlaid into the central limestone breast are polished granite pillars. It faces the former entrance to the chapel and is an original feature of the house. Unfortunately it is showing signs of weathering.

Another view of the fountain of St Patrick's College.

6   Irish Volunteer

Townland/Ward: St George's Ward
Latitude, Longitude: 53°21'37.95"N, 6°16'16.28"W
Post Code: Dublin 7

The Irish Volunteer monument is located at Blackquire Bridge in Phibsborough. It is a limestone monument incorporating a drinking fountain on both its north and south faces and surmounted by a statue of a soldier wearing the uniform of the volunteers and depicted in readiness for battle. It represents those who fought and died in both the Easter Rising and in the War of Independence.

It was sculpted by Leo Broe and unveiled in 1939 by Captain Seán Prendergast with Séamus Byrne delivering the oration. A contemporary report in the *Irish Times* estimated that approximately 3,000 people attended the event.

It is interesting, and fitting, that the sculptor himself was also a member of the Irish Volunteers.

Below the soldier are scenes from Irish mythology and ancient Irish history: the arrival of the Milesians (the first inhabitants of Ireland), Cú Chulainn fighting at the ford, and the death of King Brian Boru at Clontarf in 1014.

Phibsborough's Irish Volunteer primed and ready for battle.

The bronze plaque to the north bears an Irish inscription which translates as:

> For the glory of God in enduring memory for the officers and for the volunteers who are no longer with us that fought for Ireland's freedom and who were once members of "C" company 1st battalion Dublin Brigade of the Republican Army, a company which was founded in the year 1913.

The monument was neglected and vandalised in the 1970s, and the rifle was stolen. The soldier remained 'unarmed' until the monument was restored by Dublin Corporation in 1991.

7   Dobby Fin Millen Drill (Nightmare on Duck Street)

Townland/Ward: Grange
Latitude, Longitude: 53°24'15.32"N, 6° 9'35.01"W
Post Code: Dublin 13

This masterpiece of sculpture and symbolism is located in the ecologically and sustainably designed Fr Collins Park in Clongriffin. It was commissioned by Dublin City Council and sculpted by Alan Phelan in 2005.

The unusual and quirky inverted oil rig in the lake in Fr Collins Park.

The nearby water wall, also in the park.

The chromed steel sculpture unusually has three names, which were arrived at with the assistance of the pupils in the local St Francis of Assisi Primary School in Belmayne, Balgriffin. The children came up with a number of names and the three were kept, the descriptive one (Inverted Oil Rig), the artist's favourite (Dobby Fin Millen Drill), and the children's favourite (Nightmare on Duck Street).

The piece connects directly to the sustainable design metaphors used in the park, as the rig is notionally returning oil to the ground.

Dublin City Centre

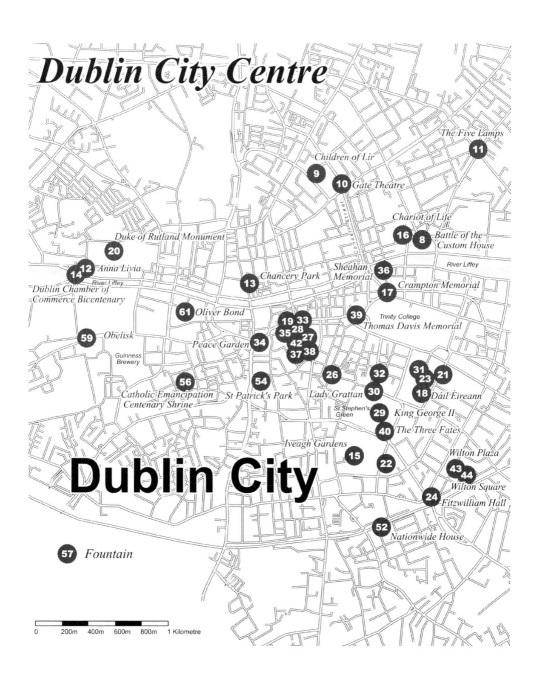

Dublin City Centre

The Five Lamps

11

Children of Lir

9

10 Gate Theatre

Chariot of Life

Duke of Rutland Monument

20

Anna Livia

16 8 Battle of the
Custom House

14 12

River Liffey

Dublin Chamber of
Commerce Bicentenary

13 Chancery Park

Sheahan
Memorial

36

River Liffey

17 Crampton Memorial

61 Oliver Bond

39

Trinity College
Thomas Davis Memorial

Obelisk

59

Peace Garden

34

19 33
35 28
42 27
37 38

Guinness
Brewery

26

32

31 23 21

30

18 Dáil Éireann

56

Catholic Emancipation
Centenary Shrine

54

St Patrick's Park

Lady Grattan

St Stephen's
Green

29 King George II

40 The Three Fates

Iveagh Gardens

Wilton Plaza

15

22

43 44

Wilton Square

24 Fitzwilliam Hall

52

Nationwide House

Dublin City

57 *Fountain*

0   200m 400m 600m 800m   1 Kilometre

8   Battle of the Custom House

Townland/Ward: Custom House Ward
Latitude, Longitude: 53°20'56.92"N, 6°15'11.36"W
Post Code: Dublin 1

As the headquarters of local government in Ireland, the Custom House was, in 1921, an important centre of British rule and therefore a strategic target for republicans.

Ireland propping up an injured volunteer.

Located to the rear of the Custom House is a large bronze sculpture and fountain commemorating the occupation and burning of the Custom House by units of the Irish Republican Army during the War of Independence.

The impressive fountain in front of the equally impressive Custom House.

While the operation succeeded, a vast number of historical documents were destroyed in the ensuing inferno, and many volunteers and some civilians were captured or killed.

Sculpted in 1957 by the Breton nationalist and Nazi Germany collaborationist, Yann Renard-Goulet, it depicts a determined, sword-wielding Ireland holding up a dying volunteer, overlooking a moated pool with cockle shell and seahorse fountain.

An inscription in both Irish and English reads:

In proud memory of Edward Dorrens, Seán Doyle, Daniel Head, and brothers Patrick and Stephen O'Reilly, who died in the Battle of the Custom House. 25th May 1921. And of the Officers and men of the 2nd Battalion and other units of the Dublin Brigade I.R.A., who gave their lives for Irish freedom.

They gave their all: may they rest in peace.

Renard-Goulet moved to Ireland after the Second World War, and was sentenced to death in his absence by a French court for collaborating with the Nazis. He spent the rest of his days in Ireland, becoming Professor of Sculpture at the Royal Hibernian Academy and a member of Aosdána in 1982.

9   Children of Lír

Townland/Ward:	Rotunda Ward
Latitude, Longitude:	53°21'12.95"N, 6°15'52.37"W
Post Code:	Dublin 1

The Children of Lír was commissioned by Dublin City architect Daithí Hanly and sculpted by Oisín Kelly. It is situated in the former Rotunda Gardens, now the Garden of Remembrance on Parnell Square.

The sculpture is formed of copper bronze on water and depicts the scene from Irish mythology of the four children of Lír being returned to human form after spending 300 years as swans.

A plaque on the wall behind is carved in both Irish and English:

In the darkness of despair we saw a vision.
We lit the light of hope and it was not extinguished.
In the desert of discouragement we saw a vision.
We planted the tree of valour and it blossomed.
In the winter of bondage we saw a vision.
We melted the snow of lethargy and the river of resurrection flowed from it.
We sent our vision aswim like a swan on the river.
The vision became a reality.
Winter became summer.
Bondage became freedom and this we left to you as our inheritance.
O generations of freedom remember us.
The generations of the vision.

It was unveiled by President Éamon De Valera on Easter Monday 1966, the golden jubilee of the Easter Rising.

The sculpture drew criticism from certain circles at the time, on the grounds that it was not fitting that a subject from pagan legend should be the basis of a public monument in a Christian country.

The mythological children of King Lír returning to their human forms from being swans.

10   Gate Theatre

Townland/Ward: Rotunda Ward
Latitude, Longitude: 53°21'10.40"N, 6°15'42.39"W
Post Code: Dublin 1

On the east side of the Gate Theatre, Ambassador, and Rotunda complex is an old drinking fountain and trough.

The forgotten and derelict drinking fountain and horse trough on Cavendish Row.

With a central half-column sculpted in the Doric style, this was a fine structure at one point. However, it no longer provides fresh water and its metal fixings have been lost or stolen.

The horse trough looking towards the Parnell monument and O'Connell Street.

11   The Five Lamps

Townland/Ward: Mount Joy Ward
Latitude, Longitude: 53°21'17.72"N, 6°14'48.10"W
Post Code: Dublin 1

On the junction of five streets – Portland Row, North Strand Road, Seville Place, Amiens Street, and Killarney Street – lies a large decorated lamp post with five lanterns and an incorporated drinking fountain on each of its four faces. This is the famous landmark known as the Five Lamps, one of the few surviving gas-lit street lamps in Ireland.

The lamp and water fountain were erected around the year 1880 after a bequest in the last will and testament of General Henry Hall directed that two water fountains be constructed in the City of Dublin in an effort to encourage sobriety among its citizens, and that a sum of no greater than £200 be spent on it.

General Hall, a native of the County Galway, had served with the British Army in India, and it is believed that the five lanterns on the post symbolise five major successes in battle championed by the British in that country.

The water originally came from the lion heads at the push of a button, with chained cups being provided for people and the basins for horses. However, today the water no longer flows and the basins have been made vandalism-proof.

The monument had a lucky escape in 1941 when German planes dropped three bombs on the North Strand area, killing twenty-eight people and destroying much of the area, but left the Five Lamps untouched.

The famous landmark of the Five Lamps in the North Strand area.

One of the now dry lion head spouts and covered basins.

12   Anna Livia

Townland/Ward: St Paul's Ward
Latitude, Longitude: 53°20'51.75"N, 6°17'25.16"W
Post Code: Dublin 7

Located in the centre of the ornamental pond in the Croppies Memorial Park, Anna Livia is an 18ft-long cast-bronze sculpture commissioned by businessman and philanthropist Michael Smurfit in 1988 in honour of his father and to mark Dublin's millennium.

The Anna Livia as seen in its original home on O'Connell Street. (Courtesy of Dublin City Library and Archives)

The Anna Livia being floated up the river it personifies. (Courtesy of Adrian McCarthy and Wildfire Films)

Its new home in the Croppies Memorial Park.

The sculptor, Eamonn O'Doherty, designed the statue to symbolise the River Liffey in female form, with long tresses of hair personifying the waves and incorporated fountains symbolising the tides. Anna Livia Plurabelle is a character in James Joyce's *Finnegan's Wake*, who also personifies the river.

Formerly located on O'Connell Street, it was removed in 2001 and placed into storage in St Anne's Park for many years while the main thoroughfare was being remodelled. Seeing its present location as more suitable, Anna Livia was partially reworked and floated up the Liffey by Ringsend Boatclub in 2011 and installed in its new home near Heuston Station.

In typical Dublin tradition, several nicknames are attributed to the monument, the most common being the 'Floozie in the Jacuzzi' and the 'Whore in the Sewer'. Such nicknames were encouraged by the sculptor, who unfortunately passed away shortly after the monument was installed in its new location.

13   Chancery Park

Townland/Ward: Linenhall Ward
Latitude, Longitude: 53°20'47.67"N, 6°16'19.93"W
Post Code: Dublin 7

Chancery Park and the adjoining complex of twenty-seven flats is a charming art-deco development located adjacent to the Four Courts on Chancery Street. It was designed by Housing Architect to Dublin Corporation, Herbert G. Simms, and built in 1935.

The simple but elegant jet fountain in the city-centre park.

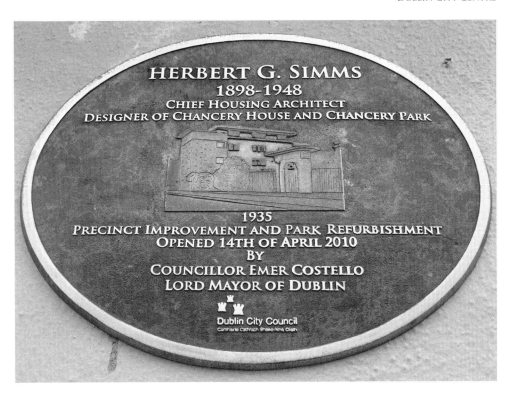

The plaque which commemorates the complex's architect, Herbert G. Simms.

The complex has received a much-needed makeover in recent years, and the park in particular has gone from a derelict waste ground to a wonderful inner-city oasis. The fountain was repaired by the Bushy Park Iron Works in 2011.

The fountain is in the form of a green bud gradually opening and surrounded by grey herons (which are actually painted white), set into an octagonal granite plinth in the centre of an octagonal pool.

The park has caused some controversy recently as its gates are locked for the majority of the week for fear of anti-social behaviour. At the time of writing, this decision is being reviewed.

14   Dublin Chamber of Commerce Bicentenary

Townland/Ward: St Paul's Ward
Latitude, Longitude: 53°20'51.29"N, 6°17'26.40"W
Post Code: Dublin 7

On Wolfe Tone Quay to the immediate south of Croppies Memorial Park lies a semi-circular fountain pool.

The fountain itself is comprised of circular granite pillars of varying heights, ascending from front to rear, each surmounted by roughly formed granite platforms from where the water gently spouts.

These pillars have come from the old estate house of St Anne's in Raheny, which was gutted by fire in 1943 and the ruins demolished in 1968. The fountain was presented to the City of Dublin in 1983 by the Dublin Chamber of Commerce on the occasion of their bicentenary and a plaque confirming this fact, with an image of the historic Ouzel Galley merchant ship, is displayed on the front of the monument.

The fountain is often overlooked as it is immediately south of the better-known sculpture of Anna Livia.

The semi-circular fountain on Wolf Tone Quay.

15 Iveagh Gardens

Townland/Ward: Fitzwilliam Ward
Latitude, Longitude: 53°20'6.90"N, 6°15'39.89"W
Post Code: Dublin 2

The Iveagh Gardens are one of Dublin's finest city parks. Designed by Ninian Niven in 1865, in an intermediate style of formal French and landscape English designs, they are unknown to many of the city's residents.

The main features in the park are the two large circular fountains on either side of the main walkway which lead to a rustic cascade of water.

The two fountains are of identical design with the water flowing from a basin decorated with a papyrus leaf motif held atop the head of a male angel whose left hand is outstretched with hand closed, and who also stands on a large serpent. Interestingly, the angel's attire is distinctly Egyptian in appearance.

One of a pair of angels that guards the fountains in Iveagh Gardens.

The two angels facing each other in their respective fountains.

The serpent underfoot.

The angel may represent the Archangel Michael and the outstretched arm may have once held a sword or scales.

Both statues are of limestone and show signs of weathering and previous repair.

Conservation work commenced in the park in 1995 and many of the built and natural features have been restored to their former glory.

16   Chariot of Life

Townland/Ward: Custom House Ward
Latitude, Longitude: 53°20'58.12"N, 6°15'18.83"W
Post Code: Dublin 2

The iconic Chariot of Life fountain was commissioned by Michael Lucey, who was responsible for the development of the Irish Life Centre on Lower Abbey Street.

Reason controlling the emotions on Irish Life Plaza.

It is a copper-bronze sculpture of a naked charioteer with horses surrounded by jets of water. It is said to represent reason controlling the emotions.

The sculpture was the work of Oisín Kelly and was unveiled on 7 July 1982 by Dr Niall Crowley, then chairman of Irish Life Assurance. Unfortunately, the sculptor died the year before this work was unveiled.

17   Crampton Memorial

Townland/Ward: College Ward
Latitude, Longitude: 53°20'44.81"N, 6°15'25.42"W
Post Code: Dublin 2

The Crampton Memorial was located on a traffic island at the junctions of College Street, Pearse Street, and D'Olier Street, where the Long Stone currently stands.

It was erected in 1862 to commemorate the life of Sir Philip Crampton (1777-1858), Surgeon-General to the British Empire, Consulting Surgeon to Dr Steeven's Hospital and the Dublin Lying-In Hospital, co-founder of the Pitt Street Institution (hospital for children), President of the Dublin College of Surgeons, and founder of the Royal Zoological Society of Ireland, the precursor to Dublin Zoo.

The highly unusual and ornate memorial to Sir Philip Crampton. (Image courtesy of Dublin City Library and Archives)

The unfortunate demolition of the unique monument that was the Crampton Memorial. (Image courtesy of Dublin City Library and Archives)

The fountain was erected in 1862 to the complex design of sculptor John Kirk and was comprised of a large ornately carved granite plinth with a drinking fountain on each of its three corners. This was surmounted by several metal animals, including a pelican and swan, which in turn were surmounted by a cascade of metal foliage into which a bust of Crampton sat.

James Joyce references the monument in his novel *Ulysses* when Leopold Bloom passes the monument and thinks, 'Sir Philip Crampton's memorial fountain bust. Who was he?'

Over its life, it had obtained several nicknames, among them being The Water Baby, The Cauliflower, The Pineapple, and The Artichoke.

It had begun to rust badly and fall apart, and an unfortunate decision was made in 1959 to completely remove it.

18   Dáil Éireann

Townland/Ward:	Royal Exchange Ward
Latitude, Longitude:	53°20'21.12"N, 6°15'12.84"W
Post Code:	Dublin 2

The fountain in front of Government Buildings on Kildare Street is usually only seen on the television. It is a large circular basin carved in polished granite and its jets spray from the perimeter into the centre.

The fountain is best seen in the evening as it is illuminated with green lighting.

Water in the halls of power. Ring of jets in front of Dáil Éireann.

19 Dublin City Rates Office

Townland/Ward: South City Ward
Latitude, Longitude: 53°20'38.16"N, 6°16'4.42"W
Post Code: Dublin 2

This wall-mounted drinking fountain is located on Lord Edward Street at the Rates Office and next to City Hall. The building was designed by architect Thomas Ivory in 1781 and built in Portland stone.

It was previously used as the Newcomen Bank, but in the 1820s it closed after the son of the founder, Thomas Viscount Newcomen, ran into financial difficulties.

The Corinthian-styled canopy of the fountain is carved into the façade of the building and a simple harp is visible in the keystone at the uppermost point. Although it is now dry, the water flowed through a lion-head spout on a cast-iron panel on the rear wall of the alcove and into a large polished pink granite basin.

The well-known drinking fountain on Cork Hill.

The crest and harp carved into the keystone about the alcove.

The fountain was renovated approximately twenty years ago and the water flowed freely for the first time in many years, but vandalism and neglect have since taken their toll once more.

20   Duke of Rutland Monument

Townland/Ward: St Paul's Ward
Latitude, Longitude: 53°20'55.99"N, 6°17'13.17"W
Post Code: Dublin 2

Charles Manners (1754–87) was a British politician and nobleman, the eldest legitimate son of John Manners, Marquis of Granby. He was styled Lord Roos, Marquis of Granby, and 4th Duke of Rutland. He held the positions of Lord Lieutenant of Ireland, Knight of the Royal Garter, and member of the Privy Council.

He personally commissioned this fountain during his lifetime and it was erected in 1785 on Benburb street outside the then Royal Barracks by the Benevolent Free Fountains Association which Manners co-founded with Sir John Blackquire.

The fountain was removed after Independence when there was little appetite for such proud displays of British ornamentation and it was reinterred inside the boundary of the barracks, with a final insult being its conversion into urinals for the soldiers.

There are plans to re-erect this once-grand fountain to its original position on Benburb Street.

Converted to latrines as an insult to the Empire.

The forgotten monument in the grounds of Collins Barracks.

21   Duke of Rutland Memorial

Townland/Ward: Mansion House Ward
Latitude, Longitude: 53°20'25.32"N, 6°15'4.13"W
Post Code: Dublin 2

The Rutland Memorial was originally erected outside St Mary's church on Mary Street (now The Church Café and Bar) but had to be removed to its present location on Merrion Square West due to the constant vandalism that it was subjected to in its former home. It was built in the early 1790s to the design of Francis Sandys in commemoration of the life of Charles Manners, 4th Duke of Rutland.

In contrast with Fountain 20, this was erected after his death, but its design bears a striking resemblance to the former.

The Duke of Rutland was a colourful character, known for entertaining and collecting objets d'art to decorate Belvoir Castle, the seat of the Dukes of Rutland to this day. His regular entertaining caught up with him at the young age of 33, when his fondness for claret lead to his development of liver disease and his subsequent death of this condition in the Phoenix Park Lodge in 1787.

This grand fountain is comprised almost completely of Leinster granite, with a mixture of Portland and Coade stone features carved in neoclassical style. It was conveniently positioned facing onto the thoroughfare here in order to allow servants from the nearby mansions to fill

The impressive memorial to the Duke.

their barrels and return home to refill the water tanks in the basements. This was common even until the late 1790s when neighbouring properties still did not have running water.

The medallions on the end piers of the fountain depict two female figures: on the left a woman in mourning with a soldier behind her, and on the right a seated Hibernia. The central arch is embellished with a Coade stone tablet, flanked at either side by roundels of the Duke and the Duchess of Rutland.

The original centrepiece comprised a very large stone shell mounted on a plinth in the centre, with a life-size water nymph sculpted in Coade stone with its arm resting on the water conduit.

The fountain was neglected on more than one occasion and became a target of vandalism on a regular basis. The Director of the National Gallery, Dr James White, had the fountain repaired as part of European Architectural Heritage Year in 1975.

It again began decaying due to lack of maintenance and repeated vandalism, and was again repaired and restored between 2008 and 2009 under the auspices of Dublin City Council by masonry conservators Interclean at a cost of €230,000.

Unfortunately, on neither occasion was the opportunity taken to restore the water supply to the fountain and the bronze lions' mouths remain dry to this day, with a pool of stagnant, stinking water in each basin.

22 ' … for peace comes dropping slow'

Townland/Ward: Fitzwilliam Ward
Latitude, Longitude: 53°20'4.90"N, 6°15'27.40"W
Post Code: Dublin 2

This fountain is located on Earlsfort Piazza opposite the National Concert Hall. The fountain represents the Lake Isle of Innisfree, so enjoyed by William Butler Yeats in his youth and celebrated in his widely acclaimed poem of the same name, from which the fountain gets its name.

It was sculpted in 1989 by Colm Brennan and Noel Kidney, and symbolises the Lough Gill island with the blue mosaic tiling representing the lake itself.

A flock of bronze pigeons fly parallel to the water and circle as if ascending into the sky.

The Lake Isle of Innisfree

I will arise and go now, and go to Innisfree,
And a small cabin build there, of clay and wattles made;
Nine bean rows will I have there, a hive for the honeybee,
And live alone in the bee-loud glade.

And I shall have some peace there, for peace comes dropping slow,
Dropping from the veils of the morning to where the cricket sings;
There midnight's all a-glimmer, and noon a purple glow,
And evening full of the linnet's wings.

Inspired by W.B. Yeats' poem 'Lake Isle of Innisfree'.

Inspired by W.B. Yeats' poem 'Lake Isle of Innisfree', pigeons fly along the cascading water.

I will arise and go now, for always night and day
I hear lake water lapping with low sounds by the shore;
While I stand on the roadway, or on the pavements gray,
I hear it in the deep heart's core.

W.B. Yeats, 1892

23   Edward Stamer O'Grady FRCSI Memorial

Townland/Ward: Royal Exchange Ward
Latitude, Longitude: 53°20'24.48"N, 6°15'11.46"W
Post Code: Dublin 2

The forgotten memorial to the once influential and controversial doctor of the Mercer's Hospital.

Born on Baggot Street in 1838, Edward Stamer O'Grady was an eminent surgeon at the City of Dublin Hospital and anatomy lecturer at the Carmichael School of Medicine.

He subsequently took up a role at Mercer's Hospital and attracted much controversy for his outspoken nature and in particular his criticism of the governors' methods, even on one occasion urging the recently widowed wife of a patient to request the coroner to enquire into the circumstances of her late husband's death 'for the sake of the other patients', as he believed that his care was mismanaged – however, a subsequent investigation proved that the patient died of simple typhus.

The following year, O'Grady gave notice of a motion: 'that in consequence of an indecent outrage by a governor on the modesty of a

One of the snarling lion head spouts.

female patient, no lay governor shall persistently dally in the female wards at unreasonable hours'. Duly outraged, members of the Board of Governors took a legal case to have O'Grady dismissed for offences 'against the duty of his office' but the case collapsed and he was exonerated when many colleagues and patients testifying as to his ability as a surgeon and his 'zeal and his kindness' to patients. After the case, the *British Medical Journal* commented 'Mr O'Grady has come out of the ordeal unscathed and with the sympathy of the public. The institution ought to be reformed and the governors could not do better than to set about this work at once'.

The disputes continued and in 1897, without notice, the Board of Governors dismissed all medical and surgical staff from the hospital, subsequently inviting them to re-apply for their jobs. O'Grady refused to leave or seek re-election and continued to administer to his patients in the wards, and began a legal case against the hospital. He unfortunately died in the same year before it could be heard.

His obituary in the *British Medical Journal* read:

No one who knew anything of him could fail to recognise his high sense of right and honour; and his dogged persistence in holding to the view which he believed to be right had much, perhaps, to do with the opinion, of those who looked at him askance. He was a generous friend of the poor, and if his friendships in the profession were not many they were very true.

The O'Grady Memorial is located to the side of Leinster Lawn and unfortunately locked away from public view due to the security needs of Government Buildings. It is comprised of a central Doric-style pillar with decoratively carved swags in Portland stone, and an elevated water basin in Kilkenny limestone. The water flowed from four iron snarling lion heads affixed to the pillar.

On the perimeter of the basin is carved: 'In memory of Edward Stamer O'Grady F.R.C.S.I. died 18th October 1897'.

24   Fitzwilliam Hall

Townland/Ward: Fitzwilliam Ward
Latitude, Longitude: 53°19'56.83"N, 6°15'9.89"W
Post Code: Dublin 2

Fitzwilliam Hall is a landmark building built in the Georgian style (although it does not date from the Georgian period). It is located on the corner of Leeson Street Lower and Wilton Terrace.

The fountain is positioned to the front of the property and along its southern boundary. It is a crisp, modern feature carved in granite and is in the style of a waterfall flowing from a protruding shelf to the rectangular basin below.

Modern and crisp on Leeson Street Lower.

25   Bord Gáis Energy Theatre

Townland/Ward: South Dock Ward
Latitude, Longitude: 53°20'37.23"N, 6°14'19.53"W
Post Code: Dublin 2

Grand Canal Square is a crisp and modern piazza designed in recent years as part of the area's regeneration project.

With the Bord Gáis Energy Theatre (formerly the Grand Canal Theatre) overlooking the area, the piazza was designed by those at Martha Schwartz Partners to be used as an outdoor stage for civic gatherings, impromptu performances, and al fresco dining.

Signifying marble rock protruding through the raw earth.

The infrastructural logistics of the piazza required as much care as its aesthetics. Situated over a previously existing one-storey parking garage, weight restrictions and venting were important factors.

The main features of the piazza are glowing, angled light sticks that evoke the excitement of opening night at the theatre. Adjacent are several unusually designed cascading marble fountains which are lit in the evening. Their triangular forms appear to push up through the ground like the geological upheaval of rock strata.

26   South King Street

Townland/Ward: Royal Exchange Ward
Latitude, Longitude: 53°20'25.94"N, 6°15'47.97"W
Post Code: Dublin 2

Installed by Dublin City Council around 2005 and shut off shortly thereafter, the Splash Pad located at the north end of South King Street has the potential to be a wonderfully modern monument which would enhance the public space here.

It has been suggested that the reason the fountain has been switched off is a flaw in its design that resulted in the water leaving the confines of the drainage area and flowing into nearby establishments.

Unfortunately the fountain has fallen into disrepair and many of the stainless steel drainage covers have disappeared, posing a clear danger to foot traffic.

Abandoned and unsafe underfoot, the Splash Pad on South King Street.

27   An Garda Síochána Memorial

Townland/Ward: Royal Exchange Ward
Latitude, Longitude: 53°20'33.93"N, 6°15'59.58"W
Post Code: Dublin 2

The sombre space which celebrates the lives of those who have given the ultimate sacrifice in the service of the people of this island.

This stone sculpture is a tribute to all deceased members of the Garda, the RIC, and the DMP.

This glass sculpture commemorates the sacrifice of the families left behind.

Located in the Dubhlinn Gardens in Dublin Castle is the Garda Memorial Garden. Unveiled in 2010 by the then Taoiseach, Brian Cowen, it honours those who died while serving on duty with An Garda Síochána, the Dublin Metropolitan Police, and the Royal Irish Constabulary. Present at the unveiling were representatives of the families of the eighty-three gardaí whose names appear on the roll of honour.

The basis for the garden is the image of a tree trunk felled before reaching maturity exposing the rings which show each year of life. The format of the fountain is a seemingly solid granite wall, pierced by a sharp glass shard, reminding us of the fragility of life.

Appropriately, the location of the garden was the place where the Garda Síochána affirmed its authority as the national police force of Ireland in 1922.

28   James A. Power Memorial

Townland/Ward: Royal Exchange Ward
Latitude, Longitude: 53°20'37.20"N, 6°16'1.94"W
Post Code: Dublin 2

There has been a fountain at this location for at least 200 years. The current fountain is a two-tiered white marble fountain set into a paved sunken garden inside the Cork Hill gate to Dublin Castle.

The fountain was donated in 1988 by the family of James A. Power, Three Bridges House, Carrick-on-Suir, in his memory, and a plaque confirms this fact.

The fluted marble finial and column of the James A. Power Memorial.

Memorial to a forgotten soul. Who was James A. Power?

29   King George II

Townland/Ward: Mansion House Ward
Latitude, Longitude: 53°20'17.37"N, 6°15'32.90"W
Post Code: Dublin 2

The two fountains in St Stephen's Green were originally built to flank an equestrian statue of King George II that formerly stood on the site of the flowerbed at the mid-point between the two fountains.

The fountains are comprised of large, circular granite-faced bowls with cast-iron representations of bullrushes and reeds in the centre, from where the jets spray. Many Dubliners will have photographs of themselves taken here as children.

On 13 May 1937 the statue of the king was blown up, leaving the two fountains flanking a void ever since.

On the day of the explosion, the *Irish Times* reported:

Early yesterday morning the statue of King George the second in St. Stephen's Green Dublin was blown up by an explosive surreptitiously placed in position during the night. Only the day before the newly crowned King, and the Queen were driving through north London where they were received with great enthusiasm. Shortly after eight o'clock a deafening explosion shattered the quiet of St. Stephen's Green, wrecking many windows in the surrounding houses and causing a good deal of distress among residents and passers-by. The bronze equestrian statue of King George the second and which stood in the centre of the Green since 1758 was blown to pieces and fragments of the granite were hurled thirty yards away.

The fountains were originally built to flank King George II's equestrian statue.

30 Lady Grattan

Townland/Ward: Mansion House Ward
Latitude, Longitude: 53°20'21.80"N, 6°15'31.62"W
Post Code: Dublin 2

This fountain was presented by Lady Laura Grattan, daughter-in-law of Henry Grattan, to the Corporation and citizens of Dublin in 1880 in an effort to encourage sobriety and assist in improving public health and hygiene.

It is carved in polished granite with a cylindrical base supporting the basin, which then rises in a quatrefoil shaft to a small Celtic cross on the top. Decorative bronze spouts are set into the shaft and chained drinking cups would have originally been attached. Flanking the structure are two rectangular granite troughs mounted on squared pedestal blocks. The nickname for the monument is the 'Horse Trough'.

Renovation works were carried out by Dublin Corporation and funded by Honda in 1992, and the fountain was restored to full working order, but unfortunately it has again fallen into disrepair. The monument is scheduled for re-location due to the current construction of the Luas Cross City extension works.

The horses will go thirsty. Lady Grattan will be soon moved to make way for the Luas Cross City extension.

31   Leinster Lawn

Townland/Ward: Royal Exchange Ward
Latitude, Longitude: 53°20'25.57"N, 6°15'12.29"W
Post Code: Dublin 2

This large water feature is located in front of the original entrance to Leinster House and facing the obelisk commemorating the first Executive Council of the Irish Free State.

It is comprised of several small jets set into a large granite cockleshell on the northern perimeter of the basin.

The water feature facing onto the Leinster Lawn.

The cockleshell sculpture which jets water into the large rectangular pool.

32   Mansion House

Townland/Ward: Royal Exchange Ward
Latitude, Longitude: 53°20'25.94"N, 6°15'29.33"W
Post Code: Dublin 2

This recently renovated three-tiered cast-iron fountain with granite basin rim is located in front of the Fire Restaurant on what is part of the Mansion House complex of buildings.

    This part of the building has recently been renovated and developed in what must be said is a modern but sensitive manner.

The Victorian fountain in the front garden of the Mansion House.

33   Millennium Garden

Townland/Ward: South City Ward
Latitude, Longitude: 53°20'38.07"N, 6°16'0.20"W
Post Code: Dublin 2

The Dublin Millennium Garden on Dame Street was located where the piazza beside City Hall is now situated.

    It was a pleasant green space and developed to celebrate Dublin's millennium year of 1988; it was unveiled by the then Minister for Labour, Bertie Ahern.

The garden comprised of a landscaped area with trees, grass, and flowerbeds with the central feature being a large circular fountain basin with three limestone statues that had originally been sculpted for one of the Dublin International Exhibitions of the nineteenth century.

In 2003, the garden was unceremoniously removed and construction of a 1,000-square-metre glass-fronted building commenced. The fountain was dismantled and the statues placed into storage.

The three statues have recently reappeared in Blackhall Place.

The three ladies that once skirted the fountain in the now demolished Millennium Garden. (Image courtesy of Maximillian Matthews)

34   Peace Garden

Townland/Ward:	South City Ward
Latitude, Longitude:	53°20'33.85"N, 6°16'16.53"W
Post Code:	Dublin 2

Located on a busy junction across from Christchurch Cathedral, this small park was dedicated to the yearning for peace in Ireland and was officially opened in 1988.

A tranquil blooming in the city. Sadly, now always inaccessible to the visitor.

The cheerful statues outside the locked gates of the Peace Garden.

It takes the form of a sunken garden, constructed in this way so as to reduce traffic noise, the main features include a bronze 'Tree of Life', a fountain and fine natural stonework of Calp and Liscannor.

Heathers provide ground cover to a backing of formal planting of hornbeams. The peace theme is reflected in both the beds of peace roses and appropriate biblical and poetic quotations from Yeats and Kavanagh. The jet used to be more elaborate, whereby a copper fixture sun from a central point, giving the water jet patterns as they flowed.

Unfortunately, in recent years, the gates to the park have remained closed, most likely as a result of anti-social behaviour that had become commonplace in the park.

35 Poddle River

Townland/Ward:	Royal Exchange Ward
Latitude, Longitude:	53°20'36.29"N, 6°16'5.32"W
Post Code:	Dublin 2

The Poddle (*An Poitéal*) is one of the best-known rivers in the city. It rises in Cookstown, Tallaght, and the majority of its course is now culverted until it finally flows into the Liffey through a large grill in the Wellington Quay wall. One of the few places to see the Poddle is inside the secondary gate to Dublin Castle on Castle Street. A small humpback bridge allows access here and a small, simple fountain is set into the exposed watercourse.

36   Sheahan Memorial

Townland/Ward: Trinity Ward
Latitude, Longitude: 53°20'49.98"N, 6°15'26.66"W
Post Code: Dublin 2

Patrick Sheahan was born in Ballyguiltenane, Glin, County Limerick, in 1876. On coming of age, he joined the Dublin Metropolitan Police and was assigned to 'B' Company in the city.

He was well known from early years for his heroism and was known, among other things, for rescuing an elderly couple from a collapsing building on Townsend Street and another time for famously wrestling with a runaway bull on Grafton Street.

On Saturday, 6 May 1905, a workman by the name of John Fleming opened a manhole cover on the junction of Hawkins Street and Burgh Quay and descended the 24 feet into the sewer below in order to repair a broken pipe.

The Sheahan Memorial is sculpted with strong Celtic revivalist imagery.

The solid Celtic cross which rises from the crown of Ireland.

Unfortunately, he was immediately overcome by gas and fell unconscious. Seeing what had happened, a newspaper boy, Christopher Nolan, ran for help and found Constable Sheahan on duty on O'Connell Bridge.

Sheahan rushed to the scene and, removing his tunic, descended into the sewer, firstly to rescue two men who had gone down in the intervening period to help but had, themselves, gotten into difficulty.

On removing them to safety, he returned to the sewer a second time to rescue Fleming, not knowing at that stage that Fleming was already dead.

Unfortunately, Sheahan was overcome by gaseous fumes and both men were rushed to Mercer's Hospital but it was too late, both had died from asphyxiation.

The funeral took place at St Paul's Retreat in Mount Argus and a funeral procession led by a mounted troop of the Dublin Metropolitan Police and followed by the bands of both the DMP and the RIC left for Kingsbridge, where the body was transported by train to Glin and onto Kilfergus graveyard for burial.

The Right Honourable Joseph Hutchinson, Lord Mayor of Dublin, opened a public subscription in 1905 to erect a memorial to the constable and the first to donate was the Lord Lieutenant, with £25. The Sheahan Memorial was unveiled by the Lord Mayor in the following year.

The limestone and polished pink granite monument displays strong imagery in the Gothic and Celtic-revival style, with a small Celtic cross surmounting the crown of Ireland, and Celtic knotwork in several places.

An Irish and English bilingual inscription on the monument states:

> This memorial was erected in memory of Patrick Sheahan, a constable in the Dublin Metropolitan Police Force, who lost his life on the 6th day of March 1905 in a noble and self-sacrificing effort to rescue John Fleming who had in the discharge of his duties descended the main sewer close by this spot and was overcome by sewer gas. It was also intended to commemorate the bravery of a number of other citizens who also descended the sewer to assist in rescuing the before mentioned, thereby risking their lives to save those of their fellow men.

37   Special Olympics

Townland/Ward: Royal Exchange Ward
Latitude, Longitude: 53°20'31.62"N, 6°16'1.05"W
Post Code: Dublin 2

The Special Olympics World Summer Games were hosted in Ireland in 2003, with participants staying in various host towns around the country in the lead up to the games.

In the southern end of the Dubhlinn Gardens in Dublin Castle is a monument dedicated to the event, and in particular to the 30,000 people who gave up their free time to assist in the organisation of the games.

Each volunteer has their name engraved on bronze plaques surrounding a square fountain with a large copper representation of the Special Olympics logo.

A wonderful monument dedicated to the selfless volunteers who gave of their time for the Special Olympics in 2003.

The names of the volunteers are forever recorded in the bronze plaques.

38 Serpent Pool

Townland/Ward: Royal Exchange Ward
Latitude, Longitude: 53°20'32.28"N, 6°15'58.36"W
Post Code: Dublin 2

A small, rectangular granite water trough is surmounted by a blue and white glass mosaic snake with its body coiled into a Celtic spiral. It has a head on both its north and south sides.

The snake's coil is inspired by Celtic imagery.

Serpentine spiral of glass.

39   Thomas Davis Memorial

Townland/Ward: South City Ward
Latitude, Longitude: 53°20'39.73"N, 6°15'37.82"W
Post Code: Dublin 2

Thomas Davis was born in Mallow, County Cork. After the death of his father, his mother moved with him to Dublin, where he grew up and was called to the Bar in 1838.

He strongly identified with Irish nationalism and co-founded the newspaper *The Nation*.

He was to the fore of Irish nationalism and was one of the pioneers of the promotion of independent Irish ideals and thinking.

He is the author of the famous Irish rebel songs 'The West's Awake' and 'A Nation Once Again'. He also wrote the 'Lament for Owen Roe O'Neill'.

Davis died from scarlet fever in 1845 at the young age of 30 and is buried in Mount Jerome cemetery.

The bronze fountain and statue on College Green were sculpted by the late Edward Delaney and unveiled in 1966 by the then Irish President, Éamon de Valera.

It depicts trumpeting Heralds of the Four Provinces proclaiming Davis's best-known poem 'A Nation Once Again'. Tablets surrounding the statues depict various harrowing scenes from Irish history.

Heralds trumpeting as Thomas Davis looks on.

One of the heralds rising from the foam so often deliberately created by the washing-up liquid bandits.

One of the several plaques which display a scene from Ireland's history.

40   The Three Fates

Townland/Ward: Mansion House Ward
Latitude, Longitude: 53°20'12.39"N, 6°15'27.64"W
Post Code: Dublin 2

This unique bronze and granite fountain was presented in 1997 to the Irish people by Roman Herzog, President of the German Federal Republic, for help given to German children after the Second World War as part of both 'Operation Shamrock' and the Save the German Children Society.

Four-hundred-and-sixty-two children were sent from Germany at the request of the Irish Red Cross and temporarily fostered throughout Ireland in an attempt to help them recover from the horrors they had witnessed during the war years in Germany.

The fountain was designed in 1956 by renowned German sculptor Josef Wackerle (1880-1959) and consists of a group of three bronze figures from Norse mythology, representing the Three Fates: Urd (past), Verdandi (present) and Skuld (future). In Norse mythology these three female figures are known as norns, who rule the destiny of gods and men.

A gift from the German people for Ireland's kindness to its children after the Second World War.

41 Treasury Holdings

Townland/Ward: South Dock Ward
Latitude, Longitude: 53°20'21.44"N, 6°14'24.97"W
Post Code: Dublin 2

In the foyer of the Treasury Holdings Building on Grand Canal Street is an impressive but simple monument of water known as a water curtain. It takes the form of a massive controlled waterfall which is maintained against the wall.

42 Veronica Guerin

Townland/Ward: Royal Exchange Ward
Latitude, Longitude: 53°20'33.46"N, 6°16'1.93"W
Post Code: Dublin 2

The grand indoor curtain of water at the Treasury Holdings. (Image courtesy of Arthur Crowley, Fountains and Décor)

Veronica Guerin (1958–96) was an Irish crime reporter who was murdered for her part in reporting on drugs crime in the capital.

Known for her insistence in obtaining primary information directly from source, she put herself in constant danger, although earning much respect from An Garda Síochána and from many criminals themselves.

From 1994, while working for the *Sunday Independent*, she reported on the proceeds of crime, drawing attention to many alleged criminals with lavish lifestyles but with no legitimate income to show for it. As a result, she received a number of death threats and warnings, but she refused to heed them.

On 30 January 1995, while stopped in her car at a red light on the Naas Dual Carriageway, she was shot several times by a man on a motorcycle and died shortly afterwards. Her work to that point had paved the way for the establishment of the Criminal Assets Bureau.

In a memorial in 1997, her husband said 'Veronica stood for freedom to write. She stood as light, and wrote of life in Ireland today, and told the truth. Veronica was not a judge, nor was she a juror, but she paid the ultimate price with the sacrifice of her life'.

The bust of Veronica Guerin with small water feature in the background.

The bronze bust and water feature located in Dubhlinn Gardens were jointly commissioned by the Independent Newspapers (Ireland) Limited and the National Millennium Committee, and sculpted by John Coll. They were unveiled by the then Taoiseach, Bertie Ahern, in 2001.

A plaque on the plinth is engraved thus:

Be Not Afraid
Greater justice was her ideal and it was her ultimate achievement. Her courage and sacrifice saved many from the scourge of drugs and other crime. Her death has not been in vain.

South Dublin Suburbs

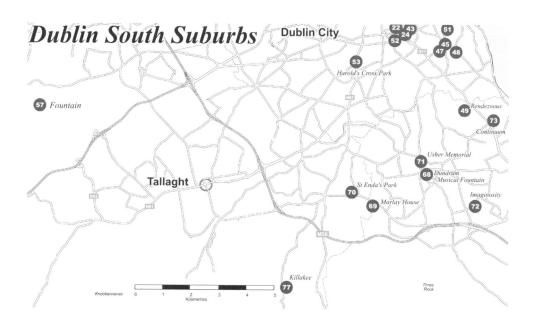

43   Wilton Plaza

Townland/Ward: Fitzwilliam Ward
Latitude, Longitude: 53°20'3.33"N, 6°14'59.94"W
Post Code: Dublin 2

This simple, quadrilateral-shaped fountain is located in the new business complex of Wilton Plaza. An interesting untitled sculpture is adjacent.

The unusual sculpture in front of the now dry quadrilateral fountain.

44　Wilton Square

Townland/Ward:　　　　Fitzwilliam Ward
Latitude, Longitude:　53°20'1.75"N, 6°14'55.58"W
Post Code:　　　　　　Dublin 2

This fine cast-iron Victorian tiered fountain was once the central feature in this triangular 'square'. New Ireland Assurance financed restoration works on it approximately twenty-five years ago and it was restored to working order. Interestingly, the water that fed this fountain came directly from the adjacent Grand Canal.

Unfortunately, it has again run dry and the basin has been planted up on a permanent basis. The planting has matured to an extent that the fountain is nearly completed obscured from view.

Renovated in recent years, but now planted up due to the lack of interest in its maintenance.

45   *Cé a dhéin an domhan?* / Who made the world?

Townland/Ward: Baggotrath
Latitude, Longitude: 53°19'42.64"N, 6°13'54.36"W
Post Code: Dublin 2

Located at the end of a small plaza in front of the Herbert Park Hotel is an interesting bronze sculpture and fountain, cast in 1996.

It is a large, circular basin with four young men lying on their backs and dressed in casual, modern clothing. Together they are holding up a representation of the globe with their feet, and it is through this globe that the water jet sprays.

The Sculptor, Clíodhna Cussen, considers herself to be at the service of the people, and makes a special effort to express in her public pieces the cultural background of the community, also evident in this piece.

This work would appear to convey the reality that it is the young and 'common person' who has made the world.

A very unique sculpture showing the youth holding up the world.

46   Overflow

Townland/Ward: South Dock Ward
Latitude, Longitude: 53°20'17.87"N, 6°14'13.65"W
Post Code: Dublin 4

This fantastic sculpture by the highly talented Linda Brunker incorporates hydrological motifs taking female form with head faced up to the sky.

   The fountain was commissioned by Cosgrave Homes in 1998 and is located on the junction of Grand Canal Street and Barrow Street. A standing female figure cast in bronze but made to appear as if it was made from the water itself. Gently curving strips of bronze indicate the ripples and reeds of water and give the figure its form. Details of fish found in the nearby Grand Canal are incorporated, particularly around the base where there is a small fountain. It stands on a circular granite base engraved with the lines from Patrick Kavanagh's poem 'Canal Bank Walk'. This line from the poem was inspirational in the concept of the sculpture: 'For this soul needs to be honoured with a new dress woven from green and blue things.'

Magic sculpture which humanises the watery element of nature.

The magical being looks to the sky.

47   Herbert Park

Townland/Ward: Fortyacres
Latitude, Longitude: 53°19'36.91"N, 6°14'4.21"W
Post Code: Dublin 4

Using surplus funds left over after the Royal Visit of George V to Dublin in 1911, Pembroke Township had the drinking fountain in Herbert Park designed by A.G. Chaytar Millar and erected by the contractor, James Beckett.

It is an ornately decorated cast-iron drinking fountain with four basins and two at its base for dogs. It is set into a large three-stepped granite podium.

Despite its poor condition, it still functions.

For the health of homosapien and canine.

48　Four Seasons Hotel

Townland/Ward:　Smotscourt
Latitude, Longitude:　53°19'35.33"N, 6°13'32.02"W
Post Code:　Dublin 4

Outside the five-star Four Seasons Hotel in Ballsbridge is a large, circular fountain with a several powerful jets. Around is neatly planted with seasonal bedding flowers and box hedging.

The very lifelike sculpture that is 'Elemental' at the Four Seasons Hotel.

The sculpture that is 'Creating'.

There are two sculptures on either side of the fountain, both by J. Seward Johnson, Jnr. The first is entitled 'Creating' and takes the form of a middle-aged man in a tie and cardigan sitting down with a pile of books and writing into another. The second sculpture is entitled 'Elemental' and is a man and woman apparently shielding from the rain under a drawn umbrella.

49   Rendezvous

Townland/Ward: Roebuck
Latitude, Longitude: 53°18'28.65"N, 6°13'17.78"W
Post Code: Dublin 4

The piece 'Rendezvous' overlooks the lake and fountains on the UCD Campus at Belfield, and is said to represent anticipation, excitement and the anxiety of an expected meeting.

In this piece, the female subject looks over her shoulder, and as she does some may see strength, whilst others may see vulnerability.

Although loosely described as figurative, his sculpture is expressionist in influence and evolves from a confident understanding of anatomy and of his medium, coupled with a quirky way of looking at life.

The narrow bronze sculpture provides an excellent place to rest and watch the lake fountains on the UCD campus.

Working from preparatory sketches, Quinn creates wax or clay original sculptures before making moulds. From these wax moulds, Quinn takes the work through the long foundry casting procedure and patination process before arriving at the final sculpture.

50   Bewley's Hotel

Townland/Ward: Smotscourt
Latitude, Longitude: 53°19'32.98"N, 6°13'27.40"W
Post Code: Dublin 4

The building that now houses Bewley's Hotel on the corner of Merrion Road and Simmonscourt Road, Ballsbridge, has an interesting history.

The large terracotta fountain originally gifted to the Masonic Female Orphan School.

Originally constructed in 1882 by Messrs Gahan to the architectural plans of McCurdy Mitchell and built at a cost of £14,986.47, it was to be used exclusively as a female orphanage to be run by the Masonic Order.

The symbolic carvings that feature in many places on the complex are typical of the order.

The beautiful three-tiered terracotta fountain which stands in front of the main building was bequeathed to the school by a Mr Sawyer. It is not clear who this person was, only that he was not a member of the Masonic Order.

Carvings on each tier of the fountain are birds, dolphins, and manservants at the base, each supporting the basin of flowing water above.

51   Ogham Stone

Townland/Ward: Beggarsbush
Latitude, Longitude: 53°20'1.80"N, 6°13'48.19"W
Post Code: Dublin 4

Ogham is the early medieval alphabet, primarily used to write in the early and Old Irish languages (fourth to ninth centuries). It is found throughout Ireland, parts of the Isle of Man, and western Britain.

The roughly carved granite pillar stone with its surface of flowing water.

The brass inserts which represent the Ogham script.

Its base pool overflows down several cascades of water.

In front of the Institute of Public Administration on Lansdowne Road, Ballsbridge, is a large roughly carved granite stone with short brass bars inserted vertically along its northern ridge.

This monument was sculpted in the 1970s by Fred Rogerson and was designed to represent the ancient Ogham stones of this land.

The brass bars set into the stone mimic the notches in the original Ogham stones and they translate from Ogham into English as 'Institute of Public Administration'. Water spouts from the top and flows down all sides of the stone, making it sheen in the sunshine, and the pool into which it flows supports a family of goldfish.

52   Nationwide House

Townland/Ward: Baggotrath East
Latitude, Longitude: 53°19'50.11"N, 6°15'29.81"W
Post Code: Dublin 6

Nationwide House, alternatively 2 Grand Parade, was designed and built between the years 1962–64 as custom-built offices for the Carroll's Tobacco Group.

It was used for the majority of its life as the head office of Irish Nationwide Building Society (INBS), and subsequently Irish Bank Resolution Corporation (IBRC).

The building is constructed of concrete and faced with Portland stone, like the earlier Busáras. The open ground-floor level was originally designed as a peaceful area accessible to the public, with small pools, fountains, and bench seating.

This area was also used for public lectures and art exhibitions.

53   Harold's Cross Park

Townland/Ward: Harold's Cross
Latitude, Longitude: 53°19'26.63"N, 6°16'44.88"W
Post Code: Dublin 6W

In 1893, and at a cost of £700, the process of enclosing Harold's Cross Park had begun. William Shepperd, designer and gardener, was responsible for the works. It was to become a 'delightful place for the masses to congregate instead of passing their time in folly', and to the joy of many, it was to become a 'people's park', that is to say a green space for the common people, especially the working class, and not a place to be gentrified by those with influence or money.

The park opened its gates for the first time on 1 May 1894, and the ceremony was officiated by Edward Fottrell, chairman of the Rathmines Township Commissioners.

The fountain in the park, noted as a 'duck pond' on older maps, is comprised of a 30ft artificially constructed slate crag with a cascade of water flowing over the edge and into the small pond below. This pond used to be much larger with the water feature flowing from a small island in the centre; however, the expansion of the playground necessitated the reduction in size of the pond. As a result of recent renovations, the fountains were exposed for the first time in years but unfortunately it was decided to have the unique basins filled in with gravel.

The small waterfall in the former duck pond of Harold's Cross Park.

54 St Patrick's Park

Townland/Ward: Wood Quay Ward
Latitude, Longitude: 53°20'24.79"N, 6°16'16.28"W
Post Code: Dublin 8

In the park adjacent to St Patrick's Cathedral are two fountains, a large jet fountain and a drinking fountain.

The large central fountain is of sculpted red sandstone with console supports at the base rising to a fine foliated bowl. The current strength of the water jet does not seem to match the grandness of the fountain.

To the west of this is a fine polished grey granite drinking fountain, made by J. Whitehead & Sons Ltd (London). It stands on a stepped octagonal plinth, with rounded stem, rising to a basin, and surmounted by a fluted urn finial.

Interestingly, the water flows from the top of the bronze finial and four bronze bosses attached to the urn guides the water into the basin at these cardinal points.

Both fountains in St Patrick's Park.

The impressive red sandstone fountain with St Patrick's Cathedral in the background.

Unusually designed polish grey granite drinking fountain surmounted with fluted urn finial.

55   North South East West

Townland/Ward: Usher's Quay Ward
Latitude, Longitude: 53°20'39.60"N, 6°18'1.77"W
Post Code: Dublin 8

'North South East West' is an interesting sculpture set into a pre-existing fountain in the formal sunken garden of the Irish Museum of Modern Art at the Royal Hospital Kilmainham.

It was cast in bronze and steel in 2009 by Linda Benglis, after she experimented with the medium of polyurethane foam and made casts from the results.

Frozen in time. 'North South East West.'

'North South East West' in the formal sunken gardens in the Royal Hospital.

It is comprised of four bronze cantilevers, which come together in the centre, and a geyser of shooting water creates a column of water, like a volcanic eruption, for periods of five minutes at a time. The water then flows down the cantilevers in the four different directions, hence the sculpture's title.

56   Catholic Emancipation Centenary Shrine

Townland/Ward: Merchant's Quay Ward
Latitude, Longitude: 53°20'25.01"N, 6°16'46.04"W
Post Code: Dublin 8

Although now a monument commemorating the centennial anniversary of Catholic emancipation in Ireland, the famous copper-domed structure on the junction of Gray Street and Reginald Street in Dublin's Liberties was originally a drinking fountain, financed by Guinness.

A fountain has been on this site since at least the mid-1800s and appears to have had a number of incarnations since.

It was renovated to celebrate the visit of Queen Victoria to Ireland in 1897, and it is likely that its present structural appearance dates from this period.

At this time, it is noted that the drinking fountain was trimmed with dolphins and herons to demonstrate its sparkling coolness. Inside was a marble surround, with the dome

Catholic Emancipation Centenary Shrine. The original canopy of the drinking fountain now serves a different purpose.

being surmounted by a brass eagle, which, tradition has it, was shot off by the Black and Tans. The delicate tracery of wrought iron has an identical twin in the Dún Laoghaire bandstand.

Since 1929, it no longer held the function of a public fountain and it was converted for use as a shrine. A statue of the Sacred Heart was commissioned and installed on a granite plinth.

The inscription celebrates this fact: 'Erected by the parishioners of St. Catherine's to the glory and honour of God and in commemoration of the Centenary of the Emancipation, 1929.'

A subsequent inscription reads: 'Restored to mark the visit of Pope John Paul II to the Liberties 29th Sept. 1979.'

57   Farmleigh

Townland/Ward: Castleknock
Latitude, Longitude: 53°21'55.24"N, 6°21'44.61"W
Post Code: Dublin 8

Farmleigh House is located on a small rise overlooking the River Liffey in the Phoenix Park. It was built as the residence of the Lords of Iveagh and was purchased from them in 1999 by the State to be used as the official Irish guesthouse for foreign dignitaries.

'Fountain Lawn' on the Farmleigh Estate.

To the north of the house, located on the aptly named Fountain Lawn, is a large circular fountain with a diameter of 69ft. To the north-west of this, along the Dairy or Cherry Walk is an ornamental gate leading to a hidden space.

This is a hidden garden of three rectangular, brick terraces descending to an oval pool in the centre with an ornamental marble fountain of carved putti figures.

The fountain here has recently been restored under the direction of OPW and the Carrara marble was exposed once more during this work. Fine topiary peacocks and spirals surround this fountain on two levels. A brick wall enclosing the garden is paralleled by a high yew hedge which leads the eye to the two conifers framing the view to the small apple orchard beyond.

Putti figures adorn the Carreara marble fountain in the sunken garden in Farmleigh.

58   Islandbridge War Memorial

Townland/Ward: Inchicore North
Latitude, Longitude: 53°20'38.33"N, 6°19'1.27"W
Post Code: Dublin 8

The informal rose garden contrasts with the formality of the remaining War Memorial Gardens.

The War Memorial gardens were laid out between 1933 and 1936 in the Longmeadows area of Dublin 8. Their purpose was to commemorate the Irish who fell while fighting in the First World War.

Work was carried out by 50 per cent ex-British Army servicemen and 50 per cent ex-Irish Army servicemen.

Its layout is of a central 'War Stone' of Irish granite, symbolising an altar, which weighs 7½ tons.

The War Stone is flanked on either side by broad fountain basins with obelisks in their centres, which symbolise candles.

In the sunken rose gardens are also two informal fountains. These areas are designed to be in contrast of the formal nature of the main lawns.

Twin obelisks centred in shallow fountains symbolise candles on an altar.

59   Obelisk

Townland/Ward:	Usher's Quay Ward
Latitude, Longitude:	53°20'35.84"N, 6°17'24.86"W
Post Code:	Dublin 8

St James's Holy Well was located outside the walls of medieval Dublin and beside the original St James's Gate, which took its name from the well.

It was the site of a significant pattern and the starting point in Dublin of pilgrimages to the shrine of St James in Santiago di Compostella in Spain. The Obelisk fountain on St James's Street is the reputed site of the well.

It was the tradition in living memory to carry coffins three times around the fountain before burial in the nearby St James's graveyard, probably a relic of an old custom associated with the holy well.

A fine feature at the base of the Obelisk to dispense water to animals.

'Keep the pavement dry.'

The Obelisk itself was designed by Francis Sandys and erected in 1790 under the patronage of the Duke of Rutland via the Benevolent Free Fountains Association. It is a tall, slender obelisk with a sundial on each of its four faces and two drinking fountains at its base.

It was restored in 1995 by Dublin Corporation at a cost of £85,000, which was funded by both the Guinness brewery and the Irish Fund for Canada.

The fine obelisk fountain is said to be the site of St James's Holy Well.

60 People's Garden

Townland/Ward: St James'
Latitude, Longitude: 53°20'58.58"N, 6°17'55.26"W
Post Code: Dublin 8

The People's Garden in the Phoenix Park is a pleasant location to spend a summer's day. On the junction of two diverging pathways is a fine example of an ornamental drinking fountain. Sculpted of polished granite, it sits on a large square granite podium, which surmounts a quatrefoil podium, which in turn surmounts an octagonal podium. Four small brass spouts, interconnected with decorative swags, adorn the central column.

The polished grey granite drinking fountain in the People's Garden.

Decorative swags adjoin the water dispensers.

61 Oliver Bond

Townland/Ward: Wood Quay Ward
Latitude, Longitude: 53°20'41.38"N, 6°16'45.45"W
Post Code: Dublin 8

Oliver Bond Flats were built on the abandoned site of Dublin's famous Anchor brewery.

In 1932, Dublin Corporation issued a compulsory purchase order on the site for the purpose of building 5,340 dwellings for 'artisans in steady employment'.

In 1933, the Official Arbitrator, Mr George Hewson, was taking detailed evidence to support compensation claims, and various persons were compensated for losses. Some of the documents produced dated back to the time of Charles II (reigned 1660–85).

The tall, octagonal, redbrick fountain enhances the Oliver Bond flat complex.

The second dry fountain in the Oliver Bond complex.

Designed by George Simms, Dublin Corporation Housing Architect, and built by Messrs Meagher and Hayes, Cork, the complex included the building of two redbrick fountains and cement fountains, designed to enhance the environment.

These fountains survive to this day although their bowls have been filled and they no longer function.

62   Bastard Son of Sisyphus

Townland/Ward: Gallanstown
Latitude, Longitude: 53°19'54.48"N, 6°22'34.80"W
Post Code: Dublin 12

Commissioned by Harcourt Developments in 1999, 'Bastard Son of Sisyphus' was the first sculpture installed in Parkwest. It was unveiled by the then Taoiseach, Bertie Ahern, on Parkwest Launch Day.

Sculpted by Orla de Brí and derived from the Greek myth of Sisyphus, who, as punishment for his arrogance, was condemned by the gods to push a large rock up a hill only to watch it roll back down, over and over again, for all eternity.

Orla's attempt was to characterise the dilemma of modern man – the idea of the endlessness of our tasks.

The impressive sculpture comprises an 8ft-high bronze male, backed by limestone megaliths, standing above a stepped waterfall contemplating the 5ft bronze ball below. The sculpture was unveiled on 21 October 1999 by the Taoiseach, Bertie Ahern, at the Park West launch-day.

Sisyphus contemplating the futility of his task.   The pretty cascading water in this stepped feature.

63 Flock of Mallard Ducks

Townland/Ward: Gallanstown
Latitude, Longitude: 53°19'47.32"N, 6°22'20.26"W
Post Code: Dublin 12

Sculpted of bronze set into a fountain, 'Flock of Mallard Ducks' was sculpted by Lloyd Le Blanc and located on Beckett Way in Parkwest. He chose a significant moment from a huge sequence of movements as the birds are surprised and take flight.

He wanted the viewer to feel what comes before and after in equal balance so that the sculpture sits at one with the landscape.

The flock of mallards taking flight.

64 Wave

Townland/Ward: Gallanstown
Latitude, Longitude: 53°19'46.25"N, 6°22'30.23"W
Post Code: Dublin 12

The sculptor of 'Wave', Angela Conner, utilises in her abstract designs natural forces, such as wind, water and gravity, to add movement to her work. Installed in 2001, this monument is a twisting, 121ft-tall, moving spiral, which took two years to create and was inspired by Islamic calligraphy and saplings blowing in the wind.

The tallest water mobile in Europe.

The fountain at its base produces a fine rainbow in the sunshine.

The tip of the sculpture, which is not powered by any motors, can sway up to 20ft in the wind and returns to its central position by way of a 10-tonne lead counterweight.

London-based Angela Conner said, 'What it came from was watching some saplings in Vermont and noticing they always re-found their sense of balance and sense of centre. That, philosophically, is something that interested me very much. I particularly like people who get into all sorts of trouble but manage to keep their own sense of centre.'

It is constructed of a steel frame with carbon fibre skin, with the fountain at its base being of granite with a marble surround.

The fine mist of the fountain was designed to create a rainbow when the sun shines.

65 Meeting

Townland/Ward: Gallanstown
Latitude, Longitude: 53°19'52.10"N, 6°22'29.39"W
Post Code: Dublin 12

Undergraduate Patrick Loughran was chosen from the final year of sculpture students in the National College of Art and Design to create a site-specific sculpture on Beckett Way for Park West. 'Meeting' represents the act of people coming together to do business.

The piece was created from polished aluminium which reflects the surrounding environment when viewed, so the viewer and business park are represented in the work. 'Meeting' is mounted on a white concrete plinth and is 10ft high.

Patrick Loughran's 'Meeting' in Parkwest Business Park.

66a Rolling Stones

Townland/Ward: Gallanstown
Latitude, Longitude: 53°19'52.73"N, 6°22'17.74"W
Post Code: Dublin 12

Both this, and the next fountain, is a most unusual sculpture. Two great spheres, one like white marble and one with a dark, slate finish, are made to roll to and fro along rails by the weight of water changing the centre of gravity inside them. Presented on a large plinth of dark granite with water running over it, they are the centre piece to the plaza in Parkwest.

Unfortunately they were removed as significant winds affected their movement. They will be re-erected elsewhere. In their place now is 'Homage'.

'Rolling Stones'. A wonderful feat of engineering ended by the force of nature. (Image courtesy of Angela Conner)

66b Homage

Townland/Ward: Gallanstown
Latitude, Longitude: 53°19'52.73"N, 6°22'17.74"W
Post Code: Dublin 12

This fountain is comprised of four stainless steel mobiles which dip and bow to the central composite stone circle. They fill the circle with water and it, in turn, tips.

This was erected on the same site as 'Rolling Stones'.

The seesaw action of Homage.

67 The Dancing Cranes

Townland/Ward: Gallanstown
Latitude, Longitude: 53°19'50.97"N, 6°22'34.71"W
Post Code: Dublin 12

Sculpted by Lloyd Le Blanc in bronze and installed on Beckett Way in Parkwest, it was his first major work to explore flight. The two Brolga cranes perform their dramatic dance on the completion of their migratory journey; although attached, the illusion is that they are not.

Cranes taking flight, giving the impression that they are not connected.

South Dublin County

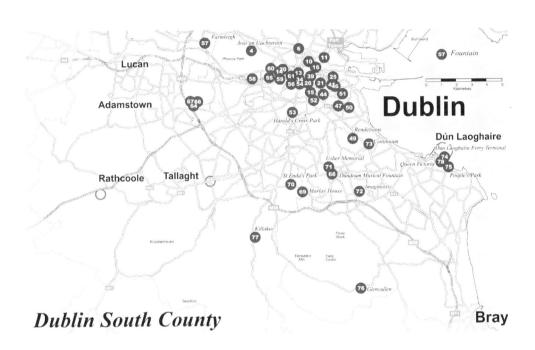

Dublin South County

Bray

68 Dundrum Musical Fountain

Townland/Ward:	Dundrum
Latitude, Longitude:	53°17'16.70"N, 6°14'33.56"W
Post Code:	Dublin 14

The Musical Fountain located outside of Dundrum Shopping Centre in Dublin is set into the old mill pond of the Manor Mill laundry which was fed by the slang river.

The fountain is a fascinating feat of engineering and electronics. It is made up of many nozzles and jets of various shapes and heights, and also hundreds of lights.

A regular display of music and lighting occurs, and the fountain's water dances to the music. It is an unusual and impressive sight.

The fountain that puts on a show.

69   Marlay House

Townland/Ward: Haroldsgrange
Latitude, Longitude: 53°16'41.74"N, 6°16'18.02"W
Post Code: *Dublin 14*

The 4.5-acre walled gardens were restored in 2000 under the Great Gardens of Ireland Restoration Programme. The gardens were traditionally divided into three walled parts, two of which are now on view.

On entering through the head gardener's house and tea rooms, the central position is taken by an attractive Regency-style ornamental garden, which boasts an extensive display of colourful period plants, ranging from herbaceous borders to shrub beds.

The orangery, arbour and water fountain combine with the other features to create a distinctive atmosphere.

The fountain in the Regency walled gardens in Marlay Demesne.

The primary figure from whose horn spouts the water.

The wet wall and secondary fountain in the Regency walled garden.

The fine central fountain is sculpted with semi-aquatic children and serpents, while the secondary fountain built into the 'wet wall' is a simple lion head spouting water into a large cockshell and overflowing from there.

70 St Enda's Park

Townland/Ward:	Haroldsgrange
Latitude, Longitude:	53°16'57.97"N, 6°16'58.00"W
Post Code:	Dublin 14

St Enda's was the location of the famous school set up by Pádraig Pearse, one of the leaders of the 1916 Easter Rising. He moved it from Ranelagh due to it being larger and also the surrounding grounds were ideal as his curriculum had a strong emphasis on nature.

Among the teachers were his brother, Willie, his sister, Mary, Joseph Mary Plunkett and Thomas MacDonagh, who were executed along with Pádraig for their part in the Rising. Fifteen former pupils were also executed.

Prior to the Rising, the basement of the school was also used as a bomb-making factory by Desmond Ryan and Liam Bulfin, both members of the Irish Republican Brotherhood.

In the park is also a number of follies, such as a fort, dolmen, Ogham stone, and arches, all worth a look.

The serpents in the column of the fountain in St Enda's Park.

The renovated fountain in St Enda's Park.

The fountain is located in the centre of the formal garden, although it was not always set into such surroundings. It is a standard jet fountain with central column decorated with serpents and dancing children.

71   Usher Memorial

Townland/Ward: Dundrum
Latitude, Longitude: 53°17'31.53"N, 6°14'44.20"W
Post Code: Dublin 14

Being the only monument in Dundrum, the Usher Memorial is located outside the Luas station in Dundrum village.

It was commissioned by friends of one Dr Isaac Usher, who was accidentally killed when he was struck by a car reversing into him near the station in 1917. It is thought to be one of the first fatalities in Ireland involving a motor car. Usher was buried in nearby St Nahi's graveyard.

The monument was set into the centre of the northern crossroads and provided drinking water to passing horses. People could also drink from brass cups that were attached to chains.

Due to the increase in motor traffic, it was considered that the fountain was blocking the road and it was moved to its present location.

During the construction of Usher House, the fountain was covered to protect it, and was hidden behind hoarding for some years but it is now back on show.

The fine obelisk which commemorates what was probably the first fatality involving a car in Ireland.

The obelisk of the Usher Memorial with Usher House in the background.

72   Imaginosity

Townland/Ward: Blackthorn
Latitude, Longitude: 53°16'39.10"N, 6°13'0.37"W
Post Code: Dublin 18

This small fountain is located in the moat at the base of Imaginosity, the Dublin Children's Museum. It is lit by LED lights which infiltrate the jets, making the entire fountain change colour.

The delightful fountain that changes colour at the National Children's Museum.

73   Continuum

Townland/Ward: Booterstown
Latitude, Longitude: 53°18'16.51"N, 6°12'21.89"W
Post Code: County Dublin

Located in the front gardens of the Radisson SAS St Helen's Hotel in Booterstown is this
bronze masterpiece by Linda Brunker.

The exquisite detail in the body of the sculpture is breathtaking.

Linda Brunker's magnificent 'Continuum' in front of the St Helen's Hotel.

Commissioned by the Cosgrave Property Group and unveiled in 1998, it dominates the landscaped forecourt of the hotel and is said to reflect the lavish interior of the historic St Helen's House. It comprises two male and two female figures, each symbolising one of the four seasons which, as if in a continuous circular movement through space, make up a sphere. They appear to be elevated by the fountains of water shooting up from below. The sculptural water feature was inspired by three basic elements of life: nature (as depicted in the decor of St Helen's), space, and the passing of time.

Each figure is made of a loose filigree of elements from the seasons that they represent:

Spring – magnolia and rhododendron leaves, sprouting shoots and buds etc.
Summer – Fig, vine, geranium leaves, clematis flower, etc.
Autumn – Maple and oak leaves, nuts, apples, pears, etc.
Winter – bare twigs, ivy, holly

The concept behind the fountain is that 'Each inanimate or living being comprises an inner motion, a succession of states, a rhythm which is their very own'.

74   Dún Laoghaire Ferry Terminal

Townland/Ward: Dunleary
Latitude, Longitude: 53°17'41.81"N, 6° 7'58.02"W
Post Code: County Dublin

The pop jet of the usually dry splash pad at the ferry terminal.

The ferry terminal at Dún Laoghaire is one of the main entry points into Ireland. Its new terminal was designed by Burke-Kennedy Doyle and Partners, and is surrounded by a large landscaped plaza with seating, palm trees and a splash pad fountain.

75   People's Park

Townland/Ward: Glasthule
Latitude, Longitude: 53°17'23.72"N, 6° 7'42.71"W
Post Code: County Dublin

The enclosed 5-acre area that is the People's Park was originally the site of a Martello tower and subsequent quarry, but was developed into its present appearance by the Kingstown Town Commissioners towards the end of the nineteenth century in the formal Victorian style.

The distinctive boy with paddle design was a good seller at the time for the Sun Foundry, Glasgow.

One of the two Victorian fountains in the People's Park, Dún Laoghaire.

It was enclosed at that time by wrought-iron railings and gates and laid out with a system of pedestrian pathways, seats, bandstand, viewing shelter, and two very fine cast-iron fountains manufactured by the Sun Foundry, Glasgow.

Both fountains, which were partially buried by the 1980s, were dug out and restored. In 1986 the fountain nearest the railway was dedicated by the Borough Council to commemorate the 70th anniversary of the 1916 Rising, with the second fountain being dedicated to celebrate Dublin's Millennium in 1988.

76   Glencullen

Townland/Ward: Glencullen
Latitude, Longitude: 53°13'19.00"N, 6°13'5.21"W
Post Code: County Dublin

This is a simple cast-iron drinking fountain with lion head spout that is a rare example of one that actually still works.

One of the few original drinking fountains in the county that still functions.

77   Killakee

Townland/Ward: Killakee
Latitude, Longitude: 53°15'10.94"N, 6°19'7.77"W
Post Code: County Dublin

The original appearance of the fine fountain in the Killakee formal gardens. (Image courtesy of South Dublin Libraries)

Killakee House was a thirty-six-roomed, two-storeyed, stucco-faced house of symmetrical aspect with a curved bow in the centre front and similar bows in the gables. It had a balustraded parapet to the roof, a veranda with slender iron uprights and a balcony above along the centre of the front, which gave the house the appearance of a Mediterranean villa.

In addition to the house, the estate comprised of huge formal gardens, a large walled garden with magnificent greenhouses and woodland walks with the Owendoher flowing through.

It was home to the Baron Massys until their ejectment from the property in 1924

All that remains of the fine fountain. (Image by Patrick Healy and courtesy of South Dublin Libraries)

on foot of a Possession Order from a Dublin Bank. It was demolished in 1941.

A large rubble column in the rear garden of the house at the edge of the woods is all that now remains of a once fine fountain which was at one time surmounted by a statue of Neptune.

Two further fountains existed in the walled garden, but these were removed some time ago, likely sold for salvage.

78   Queen Victoria

Townland/Ward: Dunleary
Latitude, Longitude: 53°17'40.27"N, 6° 8'0.46"W
Post Code: County Dublin

The image of Queen Victoria with the British crown surmounting the monument.

The highly ornate fountain on the pavillion in Dún Laoghaire.

The fine ironwork in the structure is clearly evident.

Erected in Dún Laoghaire in 1901 to commemorate the visit to Ireland of Queen Victoria, the fountain was one of a large number celebrating Queen Victoria erected in Ireland and throughout other British colonies to a standardised design by Glasgow manufacturers Walter McFarland & Co.

The fountain was seriously vandalised in the 1980s when a bomb was set off there, shattering it into pieces. It was then dismantled and placed into storage but the Dún Laoghaire Harbour Company decided in 2001 to have it restored.

It was sent to Industrial Heritage in Scotland, which owned the patents of the now disbanded McFarland foundry, and they restored it to its present excellent condition, and recast parts that could not be repaired. The mosaic was reset and the surrounding area repaved. The restoration was completed in 2003.

Technical Notes

Of the seventy-eight fountain sites documented in this book, the author has located and personally visited seventy-three of them between the years of 2012 and 2014. Of the five sites not visited, two have been destroyed and three are inaccessible.

The author has deliberately not included all fountains in the county, but rather included a selection of the most historically relevant and/or artistically interesting.

This book draws from many sources, and the bibliography at the rear lists the main references that have been used.

Unless otherwise stated, all images and interpretations are the author's alone. Full responsibility is accepted for any inaccuracies that may occur, however unintentional.

Although the water from fountains was potable many years ago, drinking from them nowadays is strongly advised against due to the likelihood that the water is polluted.

Bibliography

Anon, *The Metropolitan Drinking Fountain and Cattle Trough Association, The Historical Scene* (The Drinking Fountain Association)

Berry, Henry F., 'The Water Supply of Ancient Dublin' *Journal of the Royal Society of Antiquaries in Ireland*, Series 5, Vol. I, No. 7 (1891), p. 557–73

Branigan, Gary, *Ancient and Holy Wells of Dublin* (The History Press Ireland, 2012)

Castria Marchetti, Francesca, *Squares and Fountains of Rome* (Mondadori Electa, 2007)

Cooke, Jim, 'The Obelisks of Greater Dublin' *Old Dublin Society: Dublin Historical Record* Vol. 56, No. 2 (Autumn 2003), p. 146–60

Costello, Vandra, 'Public Spaces for Recreation in Dublin, 1660–1760 *Garden History* Vol. 35, No. 2 (Winter 2007), p. 160–79

Drew, Thomas, 'The Stolen Fountain and Rutland-Monument of Merrion-Square, Dublin' *Journal of the Royal Society of Antiquaries in Ireland* Series 5, Vol. VII, No. 2 (1897), p. 179–81

Floord, T. Donal, 'The Decay of Georgian Dublin' *Old Dublin Society: Dublin Historical Record* Vol. 27, No. 3 (Autumn 1974), p. 78–100

Hopwood, Rosalind, *Fountains and Water Features* (Francis Lincoln Limited Publishers, 2009)

Hiney, Diarmuid G., 'Only Drink and Horses: The Story of St James's Street Fountain' *Old Dublin Society: Dublin Historical Record* Vol. 50, No. 2 (Autumn 1997), p 198–9

Hiney, Diarmuid G., 'Shedding Some Light on the Five Lamps' *Old Dublin Society: Dublin Historical Record* Vol. 40, No. 2 (Spring 1987), p. 49–56

O'Cleirigh, Nellie, 'Dublin International Exhibition, 1865' *Old Dublin Society: Dublin Historical Record* Vol. 47, No. 2 (Spring 1994), p. 169–82

Scannell, James, 'DMP Casualties During the War of Independence' *Old Dublin Society: Dublin Historical Record* Vol. 61, No. 1 (Spring 2008), p 5–19

Symmes, Marilyn, *Fountains: Splash and Spectacle* (Thames and Hudson, 1998)

Tracy, Frank, *If Those Trees Could Speak: The Story of an Ascendancy Family in Ireland* (South Dublin Libraries, 2005)

Ua Broin, Liam, 'A Few Dublin Funeral Rounabouts' *Béaloideas* Iml 15, Uimh 1–2 (1945), p. 274–9.

Various, *Art and Sculpture Catalogue* (Parkwest)

Websites

www.archiseek.com

www.comeheretome.com

www.drinkingfountains.org

www.dublincitypubliclibraris.com

www.eastwestmapping.ie

www.fountains-decor.ie

www.excavations.ie

www.osi.ie

If you enjoyed this book, you may also be interested in…

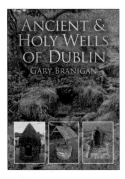

Ancient and Holy Wells of Dublin
GARY BRANIGAN

There are approximately 100 surviving ancient and holy wells in County Dublin, including natural springs, elaborate stone monuments, sea caves and hidden sites in tunnels under the Dublin streets. This book documents the remaining wells in the landscape, with many beautiful photographs of each and its surroundings, detail brief history & legends attached, and give precise locations and directions, allowing people to start visiting these ancient places of both religious and archaeological interest again.

978 1 84588 753 7

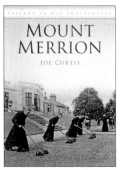

Mount Merrion In Old Photographs
JOE CURTIS

Mount Merrion lies on the south side of Dublin, 'between the mountains and the sea'. In 1711, the Fitzwilliam family walled the area to serve as their private country estate, and the 300th anniversary of this has sparked a new and enthusiastic interest in the history of the area. The early days of rustic open fields and tree-lined lanes are still in evidence, and this book by local historian and long-time Mount Merrion resident Joe Curtis continues that celebration.

978 1 84588 747 6

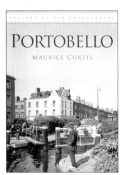

Portobello In Old Photographs
MAURICE CURTIS

In this book, Maurice Curtis, takes the reader on a visual tour of Portobello through the decades, recounting both the familiar and the events and places that have faded over time, revealing many fascinating details, including the fact that Dublin's Portobello was named after an area on the east coast of Panama! This, and much more, is captured in a timeless volume, which pays fitting tribute to this well-loved part of the city.

978 1 84588 737 7

Dublin Folk Tales
BRENDAN NOLAN

Do you know who the real Molly Malone was, or the story of Marsh's Library, or how the devil himself came to the Hellfire Club? These and many more accounts of Dubliners and Dublin City fill this book, as told by Brendan Nolan, a professional storyteller who has been recording these tales for decades. These are the stories of real Dublin, the stories that are passed from generation to generation and which give this city its unique character.

978 1 84588 728 5

Visit our website and discover thousands of other History Press books.

www.thehistorypress.ie